Tao Te Ching

A New Version for All Seekers

Tao Te Ching

A New Version for All Seekers

by
Guy Leekley

Foreword by John Friend

 Anusara ♥

Anusara ™
9400 Grogan's Mill Rd., Ste. 200
The Woodlands, TX 77380
(888) 398-9642
(281) 367-2744 (fax)
www.anusara.com

Cover Photograph: M51 Galaxy © Tony Hallas

Cover Design: Michael Wilkinson

Library of Congress Control Number: 2004104282

Leekley, Guy
    Tao Te Ching

ISBN 0-9657768-4-0

Printed in the United States of America

To Donna Limperes,
for everything

Acknowledgment

From the moment he saw an early draft of these verses, John Friend has been their tireless enthusiast and godfather. Over the years, John has encouraged me to go ever deeper into their truest meaning. His gentle, yet relentless, questioning continued to push the verses to new levels. I gratefully acknowledge his essential role in bringing this to fruition.

I also wish to thank Wendy Willtrout for her meticulous transformation of my manuscript into book format, and for beautifully implementing the complex interaction between text and graphics.

Foreword

Simply open the *Tao Te Ching* to any verse and you will find spiritual teachings offering the highest wisdom. If you continue to read through this gem of a scripture you will discover that it contains the keys to living a life in harmony with Nature. The *Tao Te Ching* has been one of my most beloved books ever since my mother gifted me with my first copy when I was just 14 years old. Now, more than 30 years later, I have enjoyed so many different translations of this treasured scripture that I have dedicated a special section of my library to it.

It was in a Chicago pancake shop four years ago that one of my yoga students, Guy Leekley, ceremoniously handed me a spiral-bound copy of his translation of the *Tao Te Ching*. Guy's luminous eyes danced with delight as he explained to me in his rich voice that his translation was the product of more than 40 years of study of the *Tao Te Ching*. He further shared with me that he first started teaching Taoism at the University of Wisconsin in the late '60s. Most interesting was his deep conviction that, in the early '90s, his life had been saved from prostate cancer largely by applying the teachings of the *Tao Te Ching* to his everyday life. Hence, I became very eager to study Guy's prodigious work and see how all of his Taoist study and profound life experiences were reflected in his translation. Moreover, I was curious to see how *A New Version for All Seekers* differed from other translations that I had studied over the years.

I opened to one of my favorite verses, verse 12, and was delighted to see that in contrast to the common translations in which our sensory experience of the material world is seen as a trap that blocks us from experiencing the world of spirit within us, Guy interpreted the ancient Taoist teachings in ways that glorified life in the physical world. It was also evident that Guy's work was more an interpretative rendering than a formal, literal translation. For example, a common translation of the first part of verse 12 of the *Tao Te Ching* reads:

> The five colors blind the eye.
> The five tones deafen the ear.
> The five flavors overwhelm the palate.

In comparison, Guy offers a very expansive, life-affirming rendering of the same section of verse 12:

> Seeing the shadow
> Around each color,
> We honor our inner eye.
>
> Hearing the silence
> Around each sound,
> We honor the inner ear.
>
> Feeling the sacred
> Around each moment,
> We honor our inner heart.

As I continued my examination of Guy's rendering it became clear that his presentation of the Truth within the scripture was composed with a timelessness that could be embraced by any spiritual seeker of any religion or philosophical system. It was clear to me that *A New Version for All Seekers* was also more in alignment with my yoga philosophy than any other translation I had ever read. I practice Anusara Yoga®, which is a hatha yoga style grounded in a Tantric philosophy that views everything within Nature—body, mind, emotions—as the embodiment of Supreme Consciousness. Within this yoga philosophy the inner, spiritual and the outer, material worlds are simply different vibratory levels of one grand Spirit. Sensuality and even desire are considered fundamentally divine gateways to experiencing and glorifying the Supreme within and all around us. Unlike many *Tao Te Ching* translations that regard these aspects of one's being as spiritually inferior, *A New Version for All Seekers* fully reflects the broad-minded and open-hearted Tantric view of life.

A New Version for All Seekers presents the ancient Taoist teachings in such a way that people of today's various cultures, religions, and philosophical paths can easily relate to them and apply them to their lives. Literal words or concepts within the *Tao Te Ching* that refer specifically to ancient Chinese government or society, such as "emperors," "ducal ministers," "rhinoceroses," or "straw dogs," have been replaced in *A New Version for All Seekers* with 21st century images and concepts that all spiritual seekers can relate to much more easily.

For almost three years, Guy and I shared an in-depth examination of the magnificent philosophical teachings of this great scripture through e-mail, phone and personal meetings in various cities around the country. Some of my most treasured times with Guy have been when he has revealed the meaning of the original Chinese characters to me as he guided me line by line through each of the 81 verses.

The ancient Chinese characters are ideograms and were never intended to be used as a spoken language. Comprised of thick brush stroke calligraphy, the characters are symbolic art representing virtues or states of mind in graphic form. In order to gain deeper insight into the archetypal meaning of each Chinese character, Guy and I would often sit in silence and meditate on their artistic form. Guy has spent many years as he puts it, "sitting with the ancient Chinese characters" and gaining exceptional insight into their deepest meanings through meditation.

For a good example of how the form of Chinese characters embodies a quality of mind, look at the watermark that represents "heart" or "the heart center" on the page for verse 12 here in *A New Version for All Seekers*. With very few brush strokes, and with none of the flowing strokes crossing each other, this is perhaps the most open and spacious character in the *Tao Te Ching*. Interestingly, the overall form of the character resembles the open chambers of the human heart. Yet more important to me is that the image evokes a feeling that represents the essence of being. Meditating on this character always gives me a spacious feeling of non-clinging freedom of spirit.

A New Version for All Seekers arises from a deep understanding of the original Chinese characters used in composing the verses. At the same time, it attempts to adhere as faithfully as possible to the traditional Taoist ideas within the ancient text. Thus, I regard *A New Version for All Seekers* as an exceptionally scholarly rendering of the *Tao Te Ching*, accessible to spiritual seekers of any religious, cultural, or ethnic background. May this extraordinary rendering of the *Tao Te Ching* bring you clarity in moments of confusion, comfort you in times of conflict, and illuminate all your days to come with the wisdom of how to flow with Nature, bringing you countless moments of the highest joy.

~ John Friend

Introduction

There are serious seekers in every spiritual tradition, and the nature of their quests varies. In some traditions, they may seek enlightenment, salvation, or the kingdom of God. Others may seek awareness of their own divine nature, or union with the One, freedom from illusion, or a life of loving-kindness.

Whatever the tradition or the quest, however, the *Tao Te Ching* offers guidance for staying on one's chosen path, abiding with the spirit of that path, and recognizing distractions that might divert us from our path.

The *Tao Te Ching* has been translated perhaps as often as the Bible or the *Bhagavad-Gita*. Its spare, enigmatic language has encouraged many translators to import images and concepts from their own cultural traditions into the ancient Chinese text. In the present translation, however, which is intended for the use of all seekers, I have tried to avoid introducing elements from any religion or belief.

The original verses of the *Tao Te Ching* were created to free seekers of that time from the bonds of rigid Confucian thought and, in general, provide poetic support and guidance for anyone serious about the spiritual life. This was done by showing us the special qualities of those seekers whose lives are truly dedicated to following a sacred Way.

The term 'sacred' is used throughout this translation to describe any way of being that is worthy of reverence and respect.

Among the qualities always seen in those advanced seekers is the way in which their actions flow spontaneously out of their own True Nature, free from delusion, fear, and compulsion.

Implicit in the original Chinese text is a belief that any of the qualities that characterize the most advanced seekers are always within the capacity of each of us. As spiritual seekers ourselves, we have a heightened awareness of their profound example. We, too, can allow our own actions to be guided by the sacred Way, open our own hearts with compassion, and fully express our own True Nature.

The three Chinese characters *tao te ching* (usually pronounced *dow deh jing*) can be translated into English as *The Classic View of Integrity and the Way*. During the thousands of years since they went from oral tradition to written poetry, the verses were sometimes known in China as the *Lao-tzu*, in reference to a mythic author of the distant past. For this version, however, the title has been left as *Tao Te Ching*, the name by which the work is known throughout the world.

Teachers in ancient China had little interest in abstract philosophical speculation. Rather than asking, "What is Truth?" they were concerned with, "How should we live?" For the past 2,500 years in China, teachings regarding the proper way to conduct one's life have been dominated by followers of Confucius, an itinerant teacher in the royal courts of ancient Chinese kingdoms.

A key concept for Confucius and his followers has been the common Chinese term *tao*, which in ordinary language means a method of doing something, or a path, a road. For the Confucians, however, the *tao* came to mean an elaborate set of rules of social conduct, customs, and institutions. Much of their writing and teaching consisted of detailed explanations and descriptions of these proper forms of social life and how those acts should be performed.

Following the death of Confucius, the influence of his doctrines continued to spread across China. After about 200 years, a few teachers were challenging the rigid, paternalistic attitudes regarding human nature and society. This small band of dissenters, now known to us as Taoists, began to look back to an older, more spiritual, meaning of the term *tao*, and they used it to designate an otherwise unnamable sacred path, or Way.

Only a few written works by those early Taoists have survived, and the best known is the *Tao Te Ching*. Within its poetic verses, *Tao* is used to represent the sacred Way, but is also used to signify a fundamental pattern of energy in the universe, energy that we can sense, but not explain or describe, and with which we may choose to align our actions. The verses suggest that this energy pulsing through all of nature is profoundly linked to the sacred Way, the spiritual path we must follow in order to experience the Source of all existence and the reality of our own True Nature.

So the opening lines of the first verse boldly announce that no *tao*, or social rules as defined by the Confucians, could ever be the true *Tao*, the sacred Way. And none of the elaborate, rhetorical language used by the Confucians could ever be considered the sacred words we use to lift us to the clarity of a spiritual life.

In a similar manner, the teachers who created these verses continued the use of other traditional terms central to Confucianism, but made it clear that they rejected the standard meanings, and were instead often using the terms to mean the exact opposite.

For example, the term *wu-wei*, which for Confucians meant inaction, or a lack of involvement, is used in the *Tao Te Ching* in a positive sense to mean a certain way of acting in the manner of a natural process. In this version, *wu-wei* is translated as 'unforced action.'

Another traditional term used in the *Tao Te Ching* with a new meaning is *shêng-jên*, which the Confucians had used to signify a wise ruler or sage, referring back to myths of sage kings. The teachers of the *Tao Te Ching* were more interested in how real people live their lives in the present moment, and they used *shêng-jên* to signify those advanced seekers of the Way who serve as our finest examples. In this version, the term is translated as 'True Seeker.'

One defining characteristic of the True Seeker is indicated in the original text by *tzu-jan* (pronounced more like *zi ran*), which has at times been translated as 'spontaneous,' and does include that quality. I understand the term more fully to mean 'our True Nature spontaneously expressing itself.'

In translating this version, I have selected English equivalents that seem to best express the meanings intended by the teachers of the *Tao Te Ching*, rather than English words that continue to promulgate the traditional meanings of the Confucians.

The Taoists who created these verses turned upside down not only the standard meanings of basic Chinese terms in their era, but the entire traditional style of expression used by the Confucians. This new teaching could not be presented properly through the usual rational arguments or in detailed explanations. That would have been an obvious contradiction of their spiritual message of joyous freedom, spontaneity and non-interference.

Instead, the Taoists could provide meaningful direction to seekers of the sacred Way only through the language of poetry. Fortunately, in the process they produced, in the *Tao Te Ching*, one of the most profound and beautiful works of spiritual guidance ever created.

~ Guy Leekley
Asheville

That which is true does not vanish; only delusion vanishes. And it is our awareness of our delusions that makes them vanish effortlessly. *Poof!*

Jakusho Kwong

Once you have given up the ghost, everything follows with dead certainty, even in the midst of chaos.

Henry Miller

Tao Te Ching

Any way that can be explained
Is not the sacred Way.
Any word that can be explained
Is not the sacred Word.

Though words cannot reveal the Source,
They do give meaning to the world we know.

To release into our boundless nature,
We must meditate in stillness.
To be free of delusion in the world we know,
We must examine our thoughts and desires.

These two practices may differ,
Yet each is a profound gateway
To the wonder of the one true Source.

2

If we think that something has beauty,
We might also think something has none.
If we think that someone is good,
We might also think someone is bad.

The idea of being requires non-being.
The idea of difficult suggests easy,
Long gives meaning to short,
While high requires a low.

When is the end a beginning?

True Seekers are wary
Of all these labels,
Preferring a Way
Of unforced action and stillness.
Then, without strain, all is accomplished.

The True Seeker is productive,
But not possessive;
Aware, but not attached;
Fulfilled, but not complacent.

We need not be concerned
About attention received by others.
Why should their status
Distract us from the sacred Way?

As we overcome greed, vanity,
And willfulness,
Our hearts spread open
And we free ourselves from delusion.

Then we gain inner strength
And act without forcing,
Leaving nothing unattended.

4

Although the Tao is formless and empty,
It never fails to provide.

The limitless Tao is there
To assist in each moment,
Softening sharp edges, releasing tangles,
Easing the glare, settling the dust.

The Tao remains deeply concealed,
Yet always available.
What could be its Source,
Since it seems to precede
Even the universe itself?

Neither the Spirit nor Nature
Has favorites.
All beings are honored equally.

Thus, the True Seeker
Does not interfere,
Allowing others the freedom
To find their own Way.

See how the space
Between Spirit and Nature
Expands and contracts like a bellows
Without ever collapsing.

Words are mostly wasted energy.
Simply maintain the still point at your center.

6

The Spirit of the valley
Is Mother to all, eternal,
And profoundly fertile.
Her energy, flowing through
Mysterious portals,
Is the source of all creation.
Sublimely subtle and continuous,
She remains effortlessly available forever.

The universe expands and contracts
Unceasingly, without needing to know
Why or how.

In like manner, True Seekers
Draw within
While remaining aware of their world.

Grounded in their Source,
They free themselves.
Secure in their core,
They flow with the Tao.

8

Be like water,
Flowing everywhere
Without striving,
Benefiting all
Without contention,
Always aligned with the Tao.

Live in touch with the earth,
Meditate deeply in the heart.

Be generous in relationships,
Truthful in speech,
Consistent in leadership,
Competent in work,
And timely in actions.

The path of peace
Is forever honorable.

Better to know when to stop
Than continue pouring until you spill.
Keep sharpening a knife,
And soon the edge is blunt.
Keep filling your house with treasures,
And soon it is not secure.
Maintain arrogance,
And you fashion your own destruction.

Simply do good work
And then withdraw.
This is the Way of the Tao.

10

While nourishing both mind and body,
Can you keep them joined in unity?
While drawing within
And following the inner breath,
Can you retain the flexibility of a child?

Turning inward to your deep, still center,
Can you fill it with the purest light?

While showing respect and compassion for others,
Can you resist interfering?
As conditions of life expand and then contract again,
Can you remain grounded in your Source?

Can this clear-eyed openness
To the ebb and flow
Be maintained without strain?

Protecting and nourishing,
Creating without clinging,
Acting without presuming,
Guiding without controlling.
This is true Integrity.

A wheel is created by attaching spokes to a hub.
Its usefulness, however,
Depends on the empty space
At the hub's center.

A bowl is created by the molding of clay.
Its usefulness, however,
Depends on the emptiness inside.

A room is formed by walls.
Its usefulness, however,
Depends on the space within.

Thus, a thing's outer form
Relies on what is tangible,
But its usefulness
Depends on emptiness itself.

12

Seeing the shadow
Around each color,
We honor our inner eye.

Hearing the silence
Around each sound,
We honor our inner ear.

Feeling the sacred
Around each moment,
We honor our inner heart.

Freed from grasping
In the material world,
True Seekers follow
Their inner light.

Freed from the bonds of delusion,
Their spirits soar.

Facing the possibility of honor or disgrace,
We feel anxious,
Since either can be lost as easily as gained.

Being so concerned for our image,
We suffer greatly, though we could
Simply let go of that concern
And all that suffering.

One who instead
Remains faithful to her True Nature
While involved in the world,
Has the steadiness others rely on.

14

We have been looking at it,
Without seeing;
We have been hearing it,
Without listening;
We have been touching it,
Without feeling.

And so we still seek the One,
Which is not brighter above
Nor darker below,
But boundless and continuous,
Pulsing through all creation.

Though it may seem elusive,
Without beginning or end,
Release now into this timeless flow
Of the present moment.
Awaken to the eternal Tao.

Since ancient times,
True Seekers
Have been subtle, profound,
And unfathomable.

They are described as:
Watchful,
As though crossing a river in winter;
Alert,
As though surrounded by danger;
Courteous,
As though they were guests;
Yielding,
Like ice at the melting point;
Solid
As a block of wood;
Empty
And receptive as a valley;
Free
As swirling water.

Who else can wait while murky water settles?
Who else can act out of deep stillness?

True Seekers
Are not attached to success,
And thus remain beyond failure.

16

By releasing completely
And cultivating stillness,
We can see how all things
Take on forms
That continuously dissolve
And then emerge again.

We can trace these forms
In all their abundance
As they appear
And then resolve themselves
Back to their Source.

This resolving of forms
Back to their Source
Deepens our stillness
And reveals our boundless nature.
There we finally release
Into illuminating Consciousness.

If veiled from this pure Consciousness,
Our experience becomes delusion,
And we suffer.

Illuminating Consciousness
Opens our hearts to compassion,
And thus to the spiritual life
Of the sacred Way.

At one with the Tao,
We can shine on forever
In the eternal present moment.

17

Our greatest teachers
Are not publicly known;
The next best often
Become famous.

Some with much influence
Become feared and scorned.
If they do not trust,
They are not trusted.

When we trust in the Way,
And respond from our own True Nature,
All can be accomplished naturally.

When our hearts are not open
To the Spirit,
Our minds turn to theories
Of honor and love.

When our actions do not flow
From an open heart,
Our minds turn to theories
Of wisdom and truth.

When relations do not flow
From an open heart,
Our minds turn to theories
Of loyalty and trust.

19

Let go of such lofty goals
As becoming holy or wise,
And we will all be better off.

Let go of righteousness,
And we will treat each other
With greater compassion.

Let go of 'getting my due'
And watch corruption disappear.

Such ambitions
Are all in vain.
Here, instead, is a teaching
To depend on:

Release all obsessions
And selfish grasping.
Locate the simplicity
Of your own True Nature.

The struggle to conform
Leads to discontent.
Approval and disapproval,
Good and bad,
All the judgments people make,
How much difference is really there?
And all those things they fear,
Why the dread?
Despair seems endless.
Yet they behave with such abandon,
As though they had little concern.

Flowing with the Spirit,
I remain apart and still,
As though I were an infant
Just learning to smile,
As though I were free
With no place to go.

While others revel in their excess,
I seem to possess nothing,
A simpleton indeed,
Out of touch with reality.
While they strut and boast,
I may seem confused, floating and blown about.
While they are busy and full of plans,
I may seem to drift.

The difference is that I am constantly nurtured
By that Great Mother, the spirit of the sacred Way.

Integrity, the fountain of all virtue,
Flows from aligning ourselves
With the Way.

Our understanding of the Way
May be elusive and intangible,
But the spirit of the Way
Is always available
To guide our awareness
Of all creation.

22

Being able to yield
Keeps us whole;
Being able to bend
Keeps us straight;
Being able to empty
Keeps us full;
Being able to let go
Keeps us new.

Content with little,
We have all that we need.
With more than we need,
We lose our way.

By following this path,
True Seekers
Set an example for all of us.
Without display, they shine.
Without righteousness,
They are distinguished.
Without boasting,
They are recognized.
Without self-importance,
They endure.
Without judging,
They avoid conflict.

Thus it remains as the ancients said,
'Being able to yield keeps us whole.'
And being truly whole,
We have all that we ever need.

23

Being mindful in speech
Is only natural.
Since nothing lasts long
Without changing,
How much is there to say?

For a life infused
With the Tao,
You must align with the Tao.
For a life infused
With Integrity,
You must align with Integrity.
Otherwise, you will only infuse your life
With discord.

When you choose to align
With the flow of the Tao,
It gladly draws you in.
When you choose to be one
With Integrity,
It gladly draws you in.
If, instead, you choose discord,
It, too, will draw you in.

Those who do not trust themselves
Will not be trusted.

Over-reaching and striving,
Flaunting achievements and boasting,
These add nothing of value
But detract from our actions.

Viewed from the Tao,
Such behavior is waste
To be avoided.

25

Before the formation
Of earth and sky,
The universe had a pulse,
Amorphous, yet complete,
Timeless, limitless, nameless,
The mother of all creation.
Let it be known as the Tao,
Let it be known as transcendent.

In its universal transcendence,
The Tao flows infinitely outward
While simultaneously drawing in.
Its energy permeates all,
Earth and sky and every being.
Thus we participate
In the pulse of the Tao.

As we align ourselves
With the rhythms of the earth,
So the earth aligns with
The rhythms of the universe,
Which in turn follow
The flow of the Tao
As it expresses its own True Nature.

Let stability be the source
Of your lightness;
Let stillness be the source
Of your actions.

Thus, the True Seeker,
Even when traveling,
Stays grounded
And not distracted by the sights.

Remain steadfast and calm.
If we lighten up too much,
We lose our base.
When we get restless,
We lose our center.

27

A skillful hiker leaves no tracks;
A skillful speaker makes no mistakes;
A skillful bookkeeper needs no calculator;
A skillful locksmith needs no key;
A skillful wrapper needs no twine.

Likewise, the True Seeker remains unattached,
Yet available to all and abandoning none.

Respecting everything,
Dishonoring nothing,
This is called
'Following the Inner Light.'

Someone who demonstrates excellence
Serves as example to those who do not.
Without respect for the teacher, however,
Or concern for the student,
Even the brightest will go astray.

One who can balance
Masculine and feminine qualities
Becomes a river valley
For us all.
Being a river valley means
A flow of unwavering Integrity,
A return to childlike purity.

One who can balance
The inner world and the outer world
Is a model for us all,
Expressing unwavering Integrity,
A return to our boundless True Nature.

One who can balance
Excellence and humility
Becomes a river valley
For us all,
A return to the simplicity
Of solid wood.

29

Straining for control
Is bound to fail.
Our world is a sacred vessel
That cannot be grasped or forced.
Interfering only makes things worse.

So accept that some will run ahead
While others fall behind.
Some moments will blow hot, others cold.
Some get strong as others weaken.
Some dominate as others succumb.

Therefore the True Seeker
Does not attempt to force results
Or to resist change.

While aligned with the Tao
We avoid aggression,
Which always turns on itself.
Thistles and briars grow
Where armies camp.
Years of calamity
Follow a war.

Fulfilling our basic purpose
Is enough.
Never push beyond that.

Fulfill your purpose
Without arrogance.
Fulfill your purpose
Without pride.
Fulfill your purpose
Without coercion.

Forced actions
Lose their way.
Going against the Tao,
They collapse.

31

Weapons can do no good
And are loathed by all creation.
Anyone following the sacred Way
Has no use for them.

Compassion and creativity
Are on the side of life.
Celebrate!
Aggression denies life.
Avoid.

While seeking serenity,
Remember that complacency
Blocks fulfillment.

The sacred Way
Is unexplainable,
Simple yet sublime,
Beyond worldly powers.

When we abide in it, however,
This follows naturally:

The Spirit descends
Into the body
Like the fall
Of gentle rain.
Life takes its course
Harmoniously,
Without rules or regulations.

Those who enforce morality,
Or try to define the Way,
Waste their efforts.

And the Tao flows on through the universe
As a river in the valley
Flows to the sea.

33

Understanding others
Requires wisdom.
Understanding ourselves
Requires an Inner Light.

Overcoming others
Requires outward force.
Overcoming our delusions
Requires inner strength.

True wealth is knowing
We already have enough.
True self-control is knowing
The purpose of our actions.
True patience is knowing
Just where our heart belongs.

Though we die,
We live on forever
Through the quality of our actions.

Any way we turn,
The Tao ebbs and flows
Through all, supporting all,
Without struggle, and without end.

Simply there, effortless,
The Tao may seem insignificant.
Yet everything that turns to it
Gains freedom.
So we consider it great –
Greatness with no attempt to be great.

35

Those expressing their True Nature
Draw others toward the security
And peace of the Tao,
Drawn as if to music or to food.
Yet any talk of the Tao seems bland
And without substance.

They may look for it,
Yet not find much to see;
They may listen for it,
Yet not find much to hear.
Stepping into its flow, however,
They find it to be supreme.

Try to limit the Way,
And it will expand;
Try to weaken it,
And it will gain strength;
Try to deny it,
And you promote its existence;
Try to take it away,
And it always returns.

Shining some light on this mystery:
Suppleness and yielding
Always overcome the forceful and rigid.

Fish have no place out of water,
And violence has no place in our lives.

37

The heart of the Tao
Is unforced action,
And nothing is left undone.

If this were understood,
People would be transformed.
In response to daily distractions,
They would turn to their still center.
Maintaining awareness there,
They could avoid diversions,
Find tranquility,
And all would be at peace.

A person of true Integrity
Does not strive for virtue
And thus can act with Integrity.
Someone trying to grasp what is virtuous
Will not act with Integrity.

A person of true Integrity
Avoids forceful action
Without even considering it.

A virtuous person
Also avoids forceful action,
But does so intentionally.

A benevolent person
Deliberately does take action,
But without personal motives.

A righteous person
Takes action
Based on personal motives or principles.

An authoritarian person
Gets others to take action for him,
For his own personal motives.

Thus,
When out of touch with the Tao,
One may seek virtue;
When out of touch with virtue,
One may seek benevolence;
When out of touch with benevolence,
One may seek righteousness;
And when righteousness is unavailable,
One may fall back on ceremony –
The outer husk of loyalty and trust.
Beyond this lies disorder and chaos.

Those with partial awareness of the Tao
May think they know
How events will unfold in the future,
But this false sense of understanding
Only leads to folly.

Instead, true wisdom is found
Deep in the meditative core
And not on the fringe of the Tao.

So center your attention,
And remain grounded
In the sacred Way.

When we first begin to view the sky
As one whole entity,
Suddenly it seems clear and pure;
When we can view the earth as a unity,
It becomes firm and stable.
In the same way, the various spirits merge
Into the one eternal Spirit;
The river valley becomes a unity,
And is seen as full and rich.

When we can view all people as one,
We see our humanity shine.

If we were to lose
This sense of unity,
The sky could dissolve,
The earth might split and valleys dry up;
Humanity might fail,
And our Spirit disperse.

Therefore,
Maintain a base of humility,
And a foundation of modesty.
By straining for attention and praise,
We lose our sense of unity.

40

The nature of the Tao
Is to eternally return,
The manner of the Tao
Is yielding.

The life of all creatures
Flows from Existence,
But Existence itself
Is grounded in stillness.

When the advanced seeker
Is aligned with the Tao,
She devotes herself to it;
Someone less diligent
May sense the Tao only occasionally;
Someone not in touch with the Tao
Laughs at reference to it.
Laughter, however, is our first step
Toward knowing the Tao.

As to the sacred Way:
Its Inner Light may seem dim,
Approaching it may seem like going back,
And its clear path may seem rough.

As to Integrity:
True Integrity may seem empty,
Great purity may seem tarnished,
And simple truths may seem to change.

The perfect space lacks boundaries,
The perfect solution is a mystery,
The perfect note awaits in silence,
The perfect image has no shape.

42

The Tao is the origin of Unity,
Which leads to Duality, then Trinity,
Then to the multitude.
These all retain the Tao's
Expansive energy of yang
And its contractive energy of yin.
When properly balanced,
These vital energies produce harmony.

Nobody desires to be isolated,
Or desperate, or needy.
Yet this is how our leaders
Often see themselves.
Thus one may lose by striving for gain,
While others benefit from loss.

True Seekers know that forceful action
Leads to no good end.
This is the essence of their teaching.

The hardest things give way
To the softest things.

Even where there is no space,
The lightness of being gets in.
From this True Seekers learn
The value of unforced action.

Teachings not expressed in words,
And the grace of unforced action,
These are rare indeed.

44

Who I am, or how I am seen:
Which matters more?
Who I am, or what I possess:
Which matters more?
Acquiring or letting go:
Which leads to more pain?

Strong attachment leads to suffering,
Accumulating what is not needed
Results in loss.

Contentment with what one has
Never leads to shame.

Those at ease within their limits
Avoid these problems and live in peace.

A great achievement is not diminished
By being seen as deficient;
Great fulfillment is not limited
By being seen as empty.

True straightness may seem bent;
True skill may appear easy;
And true eloquence inarticulate.

While activity can counter the cold,
Stillness can counter the heat.

Serenity allows us to view everything properly.

46

When the Tao prevails,
War horses are used only
To plow the fields.
When the Tao is ignored,
An army will govern.

Nothing is worse
Than not knowing
We already have enough.
No fault is worse than greed.
True contentment comes
From accepting what we have.

Without going out the door,
One can know the flow of the Tao;
Without peering out the window,
One can sense the Spirit of the Way.

The further you go
From your still center,
The less you understand.

Thus the True Seeker
Knows without traveling,
Sees without effort,
And achieves without strain.

48

Learning involves acquiring
More each day;
Following the Way involves
Releasing more each day.
Releasing and releasing,
Until we reach unforced action,
Where all is accomplished
Without striving.

Our influence on others
Should be without interference.

The True Seeker does not cling
To fixed ideas and opinions;
This allows compassion
To naturally arise.
She is kind to those who are kind,
And kind as well to those who are unkind.

To act with Integrity
Is to show loving kindness.

She trusts those who are trustworthy,
As well as those who are not.
To act with Integrity
Is to have faith in our humanity.

The True Seeker avoids diversions
And acts with compassion.
As others are drawn to her for guidance,
She remains childlike.

50

Emerging through birth
And passing through death,
Some of us embrace life
While others embrace the void.
The rest drift about,
Distracted and confused.

Those who dedicate their lives
With devotion
Can go about without fear.
Such a person leaves
No unattended opening
Available for harm.

Our True Nature flows from the Source,
While Integrity sustains us.

Indeed, the Source gives life
And Integrity nurtures it
With shelter, comfort and guidance.

Thus, all existence honors the Source
And reveres Integrity,
Not by compulsion, but naturally.

Protecting and nourishing,
Creating without clinging,
Acting without presuming,
Guiding without controlling.
This is true Integrity.

52

Everything in existence
Has a primal Source:
Think of it as a mother.
The qualities of this Source
Are expressed through all creation.
Connected to this Source,
We live our lives in freedom.

Simplify our needs and desires,
And life is continually enriched.
Intensify our distractions,
Strive for material rewards,
And our light may never shine.

Awakened to these basic truths,
We do shine.
Connected to the primal Source,
We do radiate.
Guided by our Inner Light,
We find our own True Nature.

We only require enough wisdom
To follow the sacred Way.
Our only concern needs to be
That we never stray.
The sacred Way is clear,
Though many choose the risks
Of more treacherous paths.

When our leaders are wasteful,
The fields are overgrown
And the granaries are empty.
Their clothing is luxurious,
Their equipment excessive.
They indulge in food and drink,
And acquire great wealth.
They could be called arrogant thieves.
This has nothing to do
With following the sacred Way.

54

Whatever is well-grounded
Cannot be uprooted;
Whatever is firmly embodied,
Cannot be taken away.
So be a good example
To the next generation.

Practicing this in our own lives
Develops true Integrity;
Extending it to the family
Develops family virtues;
Extending it to the community
Develops community values;
Extend it to the nation,
And the nation's virtues abound;
Extend it to all things,
And Integrity becomes universal.

View a person from that person's
Point of view;
View a family from that family's
Point of view;
The community as a community;
The nation as a nation.

And to understand the universe,
Align with the pulse of the Tao.

One who acts with deep Integrity
Is like a child in these ways:
His presence will not provoke
That which is fierce or dangerous.
His bones are pliant,
His muscles are supple,
His grip is firm.
Honoring his body,
He enjoys great vitality.
Because of inner harmony,
He knows boundless energy.

By creating such harmony in our lives,
We can experience
The One Unchanging Consciousness.
This is also known as enlightenment.

Turning to aggression, however,
Produces ominous results.
If we allow ambition
To rule our vital energy,
We exert too much force.
Then we suffer
And lose our sacred Way.

56

Someone who knows
Does not need to proclaim;
Someone who proclaims,
Generally does not know.

Can you center your attention,
Remain quiet and still,
Simplify, dim your brilliance,
And identify with the dust itself?
Then you know the Profound Unity.

This cannot be known
If you strive for intimacy or detachment,
Or for benefit or advantage.
This cannot be known if you strive for honors,
Or even if you strive for humility.

Cease striving,
And release into your own True Nature.

If you rule a country,
You must be concerned with justice.
If you command armies,
You must emphasize surprise.
But in the management of your own affairs,
You should practice non-interference.
How do I know? By observing this:

The more people are restricted,
The worse off they are;
The more they are armed with weapons,
The greater the violence;
The more cleverness and deceit,
The more dangerous the outcome;
The more laws that are passed,
The more people become criminals.

Therefore, True Seekers
Avoid forceful action,
Allowing others to transform themselves;
They protect their quietude,
Allowing others to learn tolerance;
They resist interfering,
Allowing others to find their own Way;
And they free themselves from attachments,
Allowing others to find their own True Nature.

58

When authority seems just,
People are more content;
When authority seems unfair,
People become deceitful.

The roots of good fortune
Are present in disaster;
The seeds of misery
Are present in good fortune.
So who could know what is best?
And who could know what is fair?

What once appeared to be just
Becomes perverse;
What once appeared to be right
Becomes deviant.
Confusion about this is everywhere.

Therefore, the True Seeker
Remains sharp, without cutting;
Pointed, without stabbing;
Direct, but not arrogant;
Bright, but not blinding.

Both public and spiritual affairs
Are best served with simplicity.

Practicing simplicity,
We can be aware and prepared.
Remaining alert,
We can act with Integrity.

Consistent Integrity always prevails.
Then we sustain our boundless world,
Deeply and firmly, as a mother would.

This is the Way of enduring vision
And fulfillment.

60

The way we care for our world
Should be as mindful as
The way we cook a small fish.

Approach each situation
In the full Spirit of the Tao.

The True Seeker does no harm,
So destructive forces are not provoked.
Integrity disarms them all.

When a great power is receptive,
All is drawn to it,
Like the low-lying delta of a river.
This feminine quality,
With its peaceful stillness,
Ultimately prevails over aggression.

Thus, a great power that acts with humility
Will absorb lesser powers.
And with humility, those lesser powers
Will allow themselves to be absorbed.
For each the objective
Is achieved by yielding.

When the purpose of a great power
Is to nurture others,
Lesser powers seek to belong.
Thus all can benefit
When the powerful are receptive
And promote peace.

62

The sacred Way is a shelter for all,
A home for the blessed
And a refuge for the needy.

While fine words gain esteem,
And good deeds increase our status,
Following the Way can set us free.

Even in moments of great honor,
When fine rewards are offered,
Better to stay with the Way.

Why did the ancients so value the sacred Way?
They said, 'There what you seek, you will find;
There you can be redeemed.'
Thus it was seen as the greatest of treasures.

Act without striving,
Work without straining,
Find flavor in the tasteless.
Respect the small
And value the few.

Respond to resentment with Integrity.
Start with the simple in complex tasks.
Everything that seems difficult
Begins with the easy,
And great projects are composed of small steps.

The True Seeker never bothers
To attempt great achievements,
And thus achieves greatness.

Weak commitment inspires little trust.
What at first seems easy,
In time becomes more difficult.
Thus, the True Seeker accepts uncertainty
And remains undisturbed.

64

That which is centered
Can be sustained.
That which is anticipated
Can be avoided.
Anything brittle easily cracks.
Anything cracked easily shatters.

Therefore, act before problems arise,
Make arrangements to avoid disorder.
A tree that fills the arms' embrace
Grew from a tiny shoot;
A terrace nine stories high
Began as a scoop of dirt;
A journey of a thousand miles
Began with a first step.

Interfering is self-defeating,
Willful grasping results in loss.
Therefore, the True Seeker
Does not act forcefully
And thus avoids defeat;
Does not grasp,
And thus avoids loss.

Often people fail as they near success.
Therefore, see endings as beginnings.

Embracing freedom from delusion,
The True Seeker practices a Way
That is usually ignored:
Being available
Without interfering,
As others learn to express
Their own True Nature.

65

True Seekers do not attempt
To enlighten all people,
But encourage their natural state.

When not in their natural state,
People try to be clever;
In positions of authority
They become thieves.

Those in power who can be natural
Are a blessing for all.

Being aware of these alternatives,
We can choose our own path.

Being mindful of our practices
Draws all that we are
Back into harmony.

By remaining at a lower level,
The great rivers and seas
Receive their tributaries.
Thus, one who would be a guide to others
Should be humble before them;
One who wishes to lead
Should take a place in the rear.

The True Seeker may be profound,
But never arrogant;
May be powerful,
But never harmful;
May be honorable,
But never feared.
Since she does not contend with others,
No one contends with her.

67

Anyone can recognize
The transcendence of the sacred Way.
It is totally unique.
How could it be like anything else?

We guard and cherish these three treasures:
The first is compassion,
The second is simplicity,
And the third is not presuming
That we come ahead of others.

From compassion comes courage,
From simplicity comes generosity,
From humility comes wisdom.

Those who forsake compassion
While trying to act brave,
Or forsake simplicity
While trying to act generous,
Or forsake humility
While trying to lead,
Suffer from delusions.

When compassion resolves conflict,
We express our own True Nature.

A great warrior never feels
Violent or angry.
A true winner never treats others as losers.
A true leader never puts himself above others.

This is the profound practice
Of managing affairs with Integrity.

69

The wise leader says,
I will not risk playing host
If I can choose to be a guest;
I can retreat a foot
When I dare not advance an inch.

This might be called progress without struggle,
Pushing up a sleeve without exposing an arm,
Advancing without invoking an enemy,
Being armed without weapons.

When we underestimate adversity,
We jeopardize our three treasures:
Compassion, simplicity, and humility.

Although the teachings of True Seekers
Are easy to understand and practice,
They are generally misunderstood.

Their teachings flow
From a master source, the Way.
Those who cannot see this
Remain confused.

For those who do understand,
These teachings become a precious practice;
And though the True Seeker
May dress simply,
This jewel shines in her heart.

71

Awareness of the limits
Of our understanding
Is essential to our growth.
And to remain unaware
Of what we already know
Hinders our development.

When limitations are acknowledged,
Progress has no end.

For the True Seeker,
Growth continues,
Because limitations are recognized as limitations.

If you live unprepared for change,
You are courting disaster.
You will find no security
In your natural limits,
Nor comfort with your path.

If you feel as though you need more,
You will never be satisfied.

This is why the True Seeker lives simply,
Respecting herself but seeking no honors,
Grounded in her still center.

73

Impetuous bravery is life-threatening,
Calm bravery is life-preserving.
Benefit or harm, however,
May come from either.
The True Seeker does not bother
With questions as to why this is so.

The Spirit of the sacred Way
Achieves without contending,
Responds without complaining,
Serves without reservation,
And accomplishes without forcing.

The reach of this Spirit is vast and open,
Embracing all.

Those who dread uncertainty
And impermanence
Are vulnerable to threats.
Those prepared for change, however,
Remain impervious.

Threatening forces
Will always try to exert control.
But their disturbance of the Tao's flow
Is like a novice using the tools
Of a master craftsman –
Those who do so risk great harm.

75

When taxation is exorbitant,
People go hungry.
When government is intrusive,
People get angry.

When surrounded by diversions,
People forget they will die.
Those not so distracted, however,
Create in their lives
The deepest value.

While alive, one can be flexible and supple;
After death, the body becomes stiff and hard.
Living plants are tender and pliant;
Dead ones are dry and brittle.

Thus, the rigid and inflexible
Are on the side of loss,
While the gentle, supple, and yielding
Are on the side of life.

An inflexible force never wins,
A brittle tree will snap.
The unyielding and mighty succumb,
While the gentle and supple prevail.

77

The nature of the Tao
Is seen in the bending of a bow:
The top of the bow is pulled downward
As the bottom is drawn upward.
These opposing actions respond
To changing tension on the string.

Thus the Tao constantly adjusts,
contracting and expanding
According to need.

The usual way of mankind, however,
Is to take from those who lack
And provide more for those who have.

Those living in the Spirit of the sacred Way
Divide their excess among those in need.

The True Seeker follows the Way
Without concern for results,
Without taking credit,
And without display.

Nothing is softer or more pliable than water,
Yet it excels at transforming solid stone.

Releasing instead of forcing,
Flexibility instead of rigidity.
This path is available to us
In every moment.

For the True Seeker,
To be scorned by others
Is no dishonor.
Seeing the world's delusions,
He shines his light.

79

Even when a dispute seems resolved,
Resentments may linger.

This is why the True Seeker
Attends to her own obligations
And not to enforcing those of others.

A person of Integrity performs her own duty;
Those lacking Integrity concern themselves
With the duties of others.

The Spirit is always present
To one whose heart is open.

Let there be small communities
With no need for weapons;
Let these people take death seriously,
Giving scant thought for traveling afar.
Let them keep some carts and boats,
But have little use for them.

These should be places with no show of force,
Communities of simplicity and civility,
Where food is healthy, the clothes lovely,
The customs pleasant, and the homes secure.

Although they may gaze across
At neighboring communities,
Hearing their dogs and chickens,
They leave each other in peace
And grow old gracefully.

81

Sincere language may not be sweet;
Sweet language may not be sincere.
True Seekers do not quarrel;
Those who quarrel are not True Seekers.
The adept might not be learned;
Those who are learned might not be adept.

The True Seeker does not grasp:
The more she gives to others,
The more she has for herself.
The more she provides for others,
The more she gains in abundance.

The Spirit sustains us
And does no harm.
The True Seeker lives harmoniously,
Abiding each moment in the sacred Way.

明

Thoughts

Thoughts

Thoughts

Thoughts

Thoughts

Thoughts

Thoughts

Thoughts

Thoughts

Thoughts

Thoughts

Thoughts

Thoughts

Thoughts

Thoughts

Thoughts

Thoughts

Thoughts

Thoughts

Thoughts

Thoughts